30 Day Weight Loss Daily Devotional & Prayer Book

KRISTEN KNIGHT

Copyright © 2018 Kristen Knight

All rights reserved.

Table of Contents

INTRODUCTION 5

DAY 1 – YOU CAN MOVE MOUNTAINS 6

DAY 2 – COMMIT TO YOUR PLANS 7

DAY 3 – PREPARE TO WIN 8

DAY 4 - SETTING HEALTHY BOUNDARIES 9

DAY 5 - BY HIS POWER 10

DAY 6 – YOUR ENVIRONMENT 11

DAY 7 – LETTING GO OF FEAR 12

DAY 8 – AFFIRM IN THE LORD 13

DAY 9 – KNOW YOUR MOTIVES 14

DAY 10 – FORGIVING YOURSELF 15

DAY 11 – PRAY WITHOUT CEASING 16

DAY 12 – KEEP YOUR FOCUS 17

DAY 13 – NOURISH YOUR BODY AND SPIRIT 18

DAY 14 – SPIRITUALLY ARM YOURSELF FOR BATTLE 19

DAY 15 – GETTING RID OF OLD HABITS, MAKING ROOM FOR NEW 20

DAY 16 – WHAT HAVE YOU GOT TO LOSE? 21

DAY 17 – INHALE, EXHALE 22

DAY 18 – HOW GOD SEES YOU 23

DAY 19 – BE YOUR BEST VERSION OF YOU 24

DAY 20 – WHEN TWO OR MORE GATHER TOGETHER 25

DAY 21 – ENJOYING THE PROCESS 26

DAY 22 – EDUCATE YOURSELF 27

DAY 23 – DETERMINATION 28

DAY 24 – EFFORT 29

DAY 25 - BACK ON TRACK 31

DAY 26 – STRONG FOUNDATIONS 32

DAY 27 – REST 33

DAY 28 – CELEBRATE YOUR SUCCESS 34

DAY 29 – LIVING LIFE TO THE FULLEST 35

DAY 30 – LET YOUR LIGHT SHINE 36

SCRIPTURES TO MEDITATE ON 37

INTRODUCTION

Weight loss can be difficult, and we may try many diets or new fads without maintaining results.

God loves you, and wants you to be healthy so that you can walk with Him and experience the abundance of gifts He has to offer.

In this book I hope to encourage you in Christ through daily devotions and prayers based on the scriptures, to guide you on your weight loss journey and enrich your relationship with God. This book aims to motivate you, and bring Gods loving gifts to realization in your life.

Don't give up yet!

Romans 15:13

"May the God of hope fill you with all joy and peace as you trust in Him, so that you may overflow with hope by the power of the Holy Spirit."

Matthew 19:26

".. With people this is impossible, but with God all things are possible."

Believe the unbelievable, and receive the impossible. See your potential weight loss happening for you, because all things are possible with God!

DAY 1 – YOU CAN MOVE MOUNTAINS

Matthew 17:20 He replied, "Because you have so little faith. Truly, I tell you, if you have faith as small as a mustard seed, you can say to this mountain, 'Move from here to there,' and it will move. Nothing will be impossible for you."

If you have faith as small as a mustard seed, you can move mountains! Even a small amount of faith can accomplish so much.

Rather than being overwhelmed with the big picture though, take one step at a time. Break your larger goal down to smaller goals, or 'mustard seeds'. Decide what your first mustard seed is. Is it a % weight loss? A walk once a week? Cutting out one food that you know is unhealthy for you?

Incorporate this mustard seed goal in to your everyday life, and when you are confident in it, add another. There is no need to move a mountain in one day, but as you keep pushing through your smaller goals, and as your faith in your journey continues to grow, that mountain WILL move. Jesus said so!

In Matthew 13:32, Jesus spoke about the mustard seed as being the 'smallest of all seeds', and when grown it is 'the largest of garden plants and becomes a tree'. Notice that it has to 'grow'. It does not become a tree overnight.

Prayer: *Lord, help me to begin setting 'mustard seed' goals and realize I need to let my faith grow. Teach me to grow in my faith as I embark on my weight loss journey. I believe I can move mountains!*

DAY 2 – COMMIT TO YOUR PLANS

Proverbs 16:3 Commit to the LORD whatever you do, and he will establish your plans.

Did you read that? The Lord will establish your plans if you commit!

Your first commitment doesn't need to be massive – it could be setting aside a few minutes for prayer each morning, followed by a healthy breakfast. The hard part is, you guessed it, committing! This means you have to DO the things you have committed to. EVERY SINGLE DAY. Regardless of how you feel. This is commitment.

A commitment could be to not give in to temptation. Next time you don't give in to a temptation, imagine walking around with that crown God has promised on your head! Walk proud, shoulders back, head up high – just as God wants you to!

And sure, you are going to slip up some times. This introduces the other half of commitment – getting back on track! Just get back on your bike, and keep riding that commitment race.

Commitment isn't always easy, and can also be easy to forget! So set reminders in place. Put aside a few minutes to set reminders on your phone, or write them in your calendar or diary – whatever works for you.

Prayer: *Lord, help me today to commit to my weight loss journey, knowing that this is want you want for my life. When temptations arise, I pray that You lead me in the right direction. Keep my mind on You.*

DAY 3 – PREPARE TO WIN

Philippians 4:13 I can do all this through him who gives me strength.

Today we are focusing on having yourself set up to make your weight loss journey easier on a daily basis.

One of my favorite habits is to have a full water bottle beside my bed, so each morning it is one of the first things I see. Drinking water first thing in the morning is a great set up for your day. As I leave the bedroom, I take my water bottle with me – and keep it with me most of the time, as a constant reminder to keep my water up. Having it in a water bottle also helps me keep track of how much I am drinking!

Another helpful habit I have introduced is cooking healthy food I can either keep in the freezer or fridge, ready for mealtime. I was finding that instead of eating too much, I began not eating at all as I did not have the energy to prepare something healthy, and would feel guilty for eating unhealthy foods! Not eating can have the same effect on your weight and health as overeating can - your body stores fat to keep you going, you lack energy, you get tired mid-afternoon – which can result in you reaching out and snacking on food with no nutritional value. As an example, as I write this, I have a pot of brown rice cooking on the stove. I am not necessarily going to eat it now, but it will keep in the fridge for a couple of days. I can add vegies or fish to it when I don't feel like cooking. This habit can take a little planning.

Prayer: *Lord, I am prepared to win! Guide me as I put healthy practices in to place, planning my journey to help me along every day. I can do all things through you!*

DAY 4 - SETTING HEALTHY BOUNDARIES

1 Corinthians 10:31 So whether you eat or drink or whatever you do, do it all for the glory of God.

A lack of boundaries may be the cause of why you are on this journey in the first place – so this needs to change. Whether it's boundaries with yourself, with others or with things, take a moment to reflect on those that may be slowing you down in your journey.

If it isn't helpful to yourself, others or to God, then let it go. Do not accept it in to your life anymore! You are a new creation, and have no room for it any more in your new and blessed life. Picture yourself as you would like to be in a year or two. What is stopping you from getting there? What are you saying yes to without thought that may hinder you becoming the person God intended you to be?

It could be a minor thing, like having too much food on your plate. Or could be emotional, being around negative people that drag you down, leaving you feeling lethargic or unmotivated after speaking with them.

Or it could even be people close to you that are not supportive to you on this journey. Set a boundary in place, letting them know that you do value there opinion, but that you are doing a positive thing for yourself and their comments are making you uncomfortable. If they love you, they will understand. Pray for them.

Prayer: *Lord, I know that you want me to be a healthier version of myself, and that could require me to set new boundaries. I pray that you give me strength to put these in place.*

DAY 5 - BY HIS POWER

Zechariah 4:6 '… Not by might nor by power, but by my Spirit,' says the Lord Almighty.

We all have those days where we just lack the motivation or energy to do things we need to do to continue our journey. The danger with letting it slide for a day is that it can easily turn in to two days, a week, a month – even years!

Lacking energy today? Pray about it! Ask God to help you with your motivation, and have a conversation with Him about why you embarked on this journey in the first place. He loves it when you talk to Him.

Cast all your cares on the Lord!

Take a few minutes today to thing about activities that may give you extra energy. Believe it or not, though we sometimes lack the energy to exercise, a quick walk will actually invigorate us!

Prayer: *Lord, I know you are with me on my journey. On days when I don't feel like continuing, remind me why I am on this journey, and that your Spirit gives me power.*

DAY 6 – YOUR ENVIRONMENT

Proverbs 14:15 The simple believe anything, but the prudent give thought to their steps.

Is your environment in sync with your journey? Are there temptations that may get in the way?

God will not tempt you beyond anything you can bear, but to make your journey easier, remove temptations. Think for a moment or two about temptations that could hinder you. These may be unhealthy foods that are in the house, your car or at work. It could be the amount of TV you watch – perhaps put a limit on this. If it is not uplifting or nourishing for your soul, don't watch it! Social media seems to be a big time waster for some these days.

One temptation that many of us are not aware of is negative thoughts. They drain your energy, motivation, and serve no purpose to God, yourself, or those around you. If you find that much of your time is spent in a negative or anxious frame of mind, as God to redirect your thinking.

Prayer: *Lord, help me prepare my environment to become uplifting and supportive of my journey goals. Help me in times of temptation, and bring to mind those things I can remove.*

DAY 7 – LETTING GO OF FEAR

John 14:27 Peace I leave with you; my peace I give you. I do not give to you as the world gives. Do not let your hearts be troubled and do not be afraid.

We often stop in our tracks due to fear of failure, but the bible says 'Do not let your hearts be troubled and do not be afraid'.

Just imagine how much you could achieve in the absence of fear? There are necessary fears, for example fear of being hit by a car crossing a busy street. But this doesn't mean you will never cross a street, it just means you have to follow certain rules to safely get across.

You may be fearful that you won't lose weight. But again – there are rules. Follow them and you WILL lose weight. Eating healthy, sleeping enough, getting enough exercise, relying on God – how can you fail? Only by fear or unbelief of it not working. Will you follow the rules to safely cross this street called weight loss?

Shift your thinking from fear to faith. Don't rely on your feelings, just follow the rules and believe in them. Millions, if not billions of people have done it successfully before you, so why can't you?

Prayer: *Lord, let me put my trust in you, and the process of becoming a healthier version of me. Help me to turn my fear into faith.*

DAY 8 – AFFIRM IN THE LORD

1 John 5:14 This is the confidence we have in approaching God: that if we ask anything according to his will, he hears us.

God hears us when we pray 'according to His will'. It is God's will that you live a healthy fulfilled life, and he will answer your prayers.

Commit your plans daily to God. Set time aside for morning prayer even while still in bed if that's what it takes! In Psalm 143:8 David says 'Let the morning bring me word of your unfailing love, for I have put my trust in you . Show me the way I should go, for to you I entrust my life.' Ask God for guidance in your weight loss journey, confident in the knowledge that this is His will for you.

Establish a daily prayer routine to firmly root your confidence in God on this journey.

Prayer: *Lord, assist me to make prayer a normal part of my every day life, that I may grow in confidence that this is Your will for me.*

DAY 9 – KNOW YOUR MOTIVES

Proverbs 14:30 A heart at peace gives life to the body, but envy rots the bones.

Proverbs 16:2 All a person's ways seem pure to them, but motives are weighed by the LORD.

I wonder how often we look at our motives? Today is the day to reflect on them.

Bad motives might include vanity, getting back at an ex with your new healthy figure, or embarking on this journey just to satisfy others.

Good motives include being alive longer for your family, being able to join in activities, having more energy for life and people, being a light for the world – and good motives won't fade. Keep these motives foremost in your mind, and do not dwell on negative motives. These won't last.

Keep your motives pure also brings joy to your life, and opens you up to more love, which leads to having the ability to give more love to others.

Colossians 3:17 says 'And whatever you do, whether in word or deed, do it all in the name of the Lord Jesus, giving thanks to God the Father through him.' Throughout today, reflect on this scripture. Is your action or thought in the name of the Lord? Are you giving thanks to God?

Prayer: *Lord, help me to keep my motives pure as I go through my day. Bring to my attention those that aren't, and help me to be a light for the world instead.*

DAY 10 – FORGIVING YOURSELF

1 John 1:9 If we confess our sins, he is faithful and just and will forgive us our sins and purify us from all unrighteousness.

God has forgiven you, and who are you to question Him on this? Are you greater than God, that you have the authority to place unforgiveness on yourself, or on to others?

When others hurt us, we are told in the bible to forgive them. This does not mean we are to allow them to continue hurting us. It is the same with ourselves. That niggly thing that you need to forgive yourself for? Forgive yourself- then commit to not doing it anymore. Easier said than done, and I have just put it in to one sentence! Forgiving can take some work - and please work on forgiving yourself first. This will open you up and make it much easier to forgive others. You may even find you no longer need to forgive certain people, as you can see the fault was in fact yours! (Don't close the book on me here!).

James 5:16 Therefore confess your sins to each other and pray for each other so that you may be healed. The prayer of a righteous person is powerful and effective.

Prayer: *Lord, I will confess my sins to You, and seek your forgiveness. I know You are faithful and just to forgive me. I am a new creation in You.*

DAY 11 – PRAY WITHOUT CEASING

1 Chronicles 16:11 Look to the LORD and his strength; seek his face always.

Matthew 7:7 Ask and it will be given to you; seek and you will find; knock and the door will be opened to you.

Conversations with God and prayer throughout your day will keep you mindful of the plans God has for you, and keep you focused on your path. God is right beside you, all the time!

Knowing that He is there will help you to make healthier decisions when it comes to your weight loss journey, and make you stronger when it comes to resisting temptation.

You can pray wherever you are, and however you like, God is listening. It may be in the car, or while going for a walk. It could be quiet reflection time that you have set aside in your day. Whatever works for you!

Prayer: *Lord, remind me throughout the day that You are right beside me, every step of the way. Help me to make talking with You a regular part of my day.*

DAY 12 – KEEP YOUR FOCUS

John 14:15 If you love me, keep my commands.

Your journey is a priority. We have many priorities, and your weight loss journey needs to be one of them. Look at how you use your days at the moment, and what you prioritize. Are they good for you and those around you? Are they helpful? Are they necessary? If not, get rid of them, or cut them down at least.

In todays society, it is very easy to become sidetracked. Keeping your focus requires you to look straight ahead at our journey, and only incorporate things that are helpful in you attaining your goal. This does not mean to shut everything else out completely – we still have friends, family and the community to look out for. Incorporate these activities where possible in line with your goals. Remember, if it's not helping you or others, you don't need it, and it will only distract you.

Prayer: *Lord, help me to stay focused this week, keeping my actions and words in line with my journeys goals. Help me to be a beacon of light for You while I maintain this focus.*

DAY 13 – NOURISH YOUR BODY AND SPIRIT

1 Timothy 4:8 For physical training is of some value, but godliness has value for all things, holding promise for both the present life and the life to come.

As important as it is to nourish you body with healthy food, exercise and rest, so it is with nourishing your spirit.

Food for your spirit can be found in the scriptures, reading and learning each day. Exercise for your spirit can be done by putting these learned things in to practice in your every day life. Rest for your spirt involves meditation and quiet prayer times.

Make time in your day to nourish your spirit, and this will invigorate your body. Perhaps read and study one scripture a day to begin with. Put these new found teachings in to practice throughout the day. Meditation and quiet prayer can be a great way to settle down at the end of the day, preparing your body for a good nights sleep.

Prayer: *Lord, I pray that I am aware of nourishing my spirit while I am also nourishing my body. Help me to learn that these two coincide, nourishing one will help nourish the other.*

DAY 14 – SPIRITUALLY ARM YOURSELF FOR BATTLE

Ephesians 6:10-11 Finally, be strong in the Lord and in his mighty power. Put on the full armor of God, so that you can take your stand against the devil's schemes.

There will be days when the weight loss journey is not as easy as we'd like – let's not kid ourselves on this one. Spiritually arming yourself in preparation for temptations, that may arise from friends, family, advertising, smells, environments- triggers can come from anywhere – will ensure you stand firm in your new beliefs about yourself and your commitment to yourself and God.

John 10:10 says 'The thief comes only to steal and kill and destroy; I have come that they may have life, and have it to the full'. Sounds harsh when we are only talking about that cute cream bun in the shop window, or that pizza that is only a phone call away. But think about it deeper than that. What will giving in to that temptation lead to? It will **steal** your focus, **kill** your motivation to keep going and **destroy** the hard work you have already put in. God wants you to have life, and live it 'more abundantly'.

Prayer is always a good first counter attack in your battle. Not only are you relying on God in this 'very present time of trouble', but it is also bringing your awareness back to Him, rather than the unimportant temptations that have presented themselves.

Prayer: *Lord, prepare me for this weight loss battle, that I will be strong in You and in Your mighty power. Remind me to rely on you in times of trouble.*

DAY 15 – GETTING RID OF OLD HABITS, MAKING ROOM FOR NEW

Matthew 16:25 For whoever wants to save their life will lose it, but whoever loses their life for me will find it.

Ridding yourself of all of your old habits in one go is nearly impossible, and we can get disheartened and give up all too soon – it can be very overwhelming! So start small. If you are currently not exercising – start with 5 minutes a day. This could be a gentle walk, or some weights, or even just 5 minutes of focusing on stretching.

If you are not eating properly, try and introduce at least one (or one more) fruit or vegetable into your day.

If you miss a day, do not get disheartened, just pick up where you left off.

Try and do the above for 1 week in a row, then 2 weeks. Pretty soon, you have formed new healthy habits! It's that easy.

If you are already exercising, and eating healthy – that's great! You are on your way to developing new habits for a new you. Continue these habits, and build on them slowly, adding a little more exercise, and healthy foods. This may include something as simple as adding an extra glass of water to your day – especially beneficial in the morning. Be transformed from the inside out.

Prayer: *Lord, I know new habits can take a little time to form. Help me to put small steps in place, and to continue these steps with Your love and will for me. Remind me, when I lose track, to pick up from where I have left off.*

DAY 16 – WHAT HAVE YOU GOT TO LOSE?

2 Corinthians 5:17 Therefore, if anyone is in Christ, the new creation has come: The old has gone, the new is here!

How exciting! If anyone is in Christ, they are a new creation! The process has already started without you having to lift a finger.

Think about the old you, what makes you not feel good about yourself? Would you be happy to be rid of these things?

Now think about this: What does this new creation look like? How does this new person feel, think and act?

So, what have you got to lose? You are entering in to a new creation phase of your life, a beautiful butterfly evolving from a caterpillar. You are now opening your wings up, inviting more freedom, joy, love and excitement in to your life. You are developing into this beautiful new creation with God by your side, every wing flutter of the way. Thank the Lord today for this wonderful opportunity He has given you to live your life more fully, while deepening your relationship with Him. What a gift!

Prayer: *Lord, remind me today that the old will pass away, and I am stepping in to a new and much better life for Your glory.*

DAY 17 – INHALE, EXHALE

Psalm 145:5 They speak of the glorious splendor of your majesty – and I will meditate on your wonderful works.

Your emotions and thoughts affect your body, and your motivation to continue your journey.

Find a quiet place where you won't be interrupted. Sit or lie comfortably. Take 5 deep slow breaths. Ask the Lord to relax your mind, end the chatter, and just focus on Him. Think about the love God has for you, and how he wants you to be happy and healthy. Think about what this would look like. What makes you smile? When do you feel your healthiest?

Good scriptures to meditate on:

Proverbs 21:21 Whoever pursues righteousness and love finds life, prosperity and honor.

2 Chronicles 15:7 But as for you, be strong and do not give up, for your work will be rewarded.

Colossians 3:23-24 Whatever you do, work at it with all your heart, as working for the Lord, not for human masters, since you know that you will receive an inheritance.

Prayer: *Lord, help me to find quiet times throughout my day to meditate on your Word. Let me find peace in my conversations with you.*

DAY 18 – HOW GOD SEES YOU

John 15:16 You did not choose me, but I chose you and appointed you so that you might go and bear fruit – fruit that will last – and so whatever you ask in my name, the Father will give to you.

God chose you, you didn't choose Him. God loves you

We often view ourselves as the we think the world views us. What if we based our self-worth on how God sees us? Take a moment with the Lord, and feel the love He has for you.

When your self-worth hits rock bottom, remember 1 Peter 5:6-7 'Humble yourselves, therefore, under God's mighty hand, that he may lift you up in due time. Cast all your anxiety on him, because he cares for you'. Notice that it mentions humbling yourself. If God cares for you, who are you to doubt this?

Ephesians 1:11-12 says 'In him we were also chosen, having been predestined according to the plan of him who works out everything in conformity with the purpose of his will, in order that we, who were the first to put our hope in Christ, might be for the praise of his glory.'

Prayer: *Lord, help me to realize that by humbling myself, and my opinion of myself, I will be open to seeing myself as You see me. You love me, and have appointed me to bear your fruit.*

DAY 19 – BE YOUR BEST VERSION OF YOU

Proverbs 27:19 As water reflects the face, so one's life reflects the heart.

You are special and unique. The bible says 'you are purposefully and wonderfully made'.

Be your best version of you – not shaped by the version of yourself that you see today. Look inside yourself, at your best qualities and make a list of at least 5, more if you can! See how you can be an example of Christ and serve the Lord with the gifts he has given YOU.

Then BE these qualities - focus on them and keep them in your thoughts and prayers constantly.

What good is it to be healthy, have lost the weight, but still have the emotional and spiritual baggage on your back from before? Lighten that weight too!

Mark 7:15 says '"Nothing outside a person can defile them by going into them. Rather, it is what comes out of a person that defiles them.".' Jesus continues in the following scriptures to explain that anything that enters the stomach can be 'eliminated' or gotten rid of, but that which is in our heart can only cause damage. You are on track with eliminating the bad influences from entering your body by eating healthier. Are you on track with what is coming out of your heart?

Prayer: *Lord, I realize that my life reflects my heart. Help me to nourish my heart, and be mindful of what I am feeding it. Fill my heart with Your love, that I may see others and myself as You do.*

DAY 20 – WHEN TWO OR MORE GATHER TOGETHER

Proverbs 15:22 Plans fail for lack of counsel, but with many advisers they succeed.

There are many more scriptures in the bible about being around like minded people, and for good reason. God does not want us to take this journey on our own, and scriptures show that there is power in numbers. Not only can you seek advice from others who have been on a similar journey, perhaps opening you up to ideas you hadn't thought of before, but there is also a feeling of support and security when you are around like minded people. And let's not forget about that dreaded word – ACCOUNTABILITY! Proverbs 27:17 says 'As iron sharpens iron, so one person sharpens another'.

If you already have a good network of friends, make sure you tap in to this while on your journey.

If you find social situations are not the norm for you, think about getting involved with one or two of the following:

- Local walking groups
- Bible study groups
- Church Groups
- Volunteering

Prayer: *Lord, help me to find like-minded people to help me continue on my journey, that I may also help them in theirs.*

DAY 21 – ENJOYING THE PROCESS

Proverbs 17:22 A cheerful heart is good medicine, but a crushed spirit dries up the bones.

'A cheerful heart is good medicine' - Isn't that exciting? We are meant to be happy, what is there not to be joyful about that!

Which parts of your journey do you most enjoy? Have you even thought about which parts you enjoy, or have you just been going through the process because you are 'meant' to?

Try incorporating things that you enjoy in to your every day journey. Do you enjoy catching up with friends for a coffee? Get a group together, or even one or two others, and walk to the coffee shop. Enjoy the cinemas? Jump on a bicycle to get yourself there. If you have children, they can get involved in these too!

Maybe there's a favorite music you like? Get your headphones out and listen as you exercise – this may involve dancing and singing around your house. Who cares! If you enjoy it, then do it!

Life doesn't need to be drab, dreary and drama filled. Start enjoying, and loving, your new life.

The joy of the lord is my strength!

Prayer: *Lord, there is so much joy to be experienced as I continue on this journey with You. Remind me each day to be thankful, grow stronger in Your joy, and praise Your name!*

DAY 22 – EDUCATE YOURSELF

Psalm 25:4 Show me your ways, Lord, teach me your paths.

In this day and age, we have so much access to information! Don't know where to start? Here's a few ideas:

- Reading the bible

- Testimonials from others who have been through, or who are currently on, this journey.

- Books – this doesn't have to be expensive, there are many books on weight loss, healthy eating and self-esteem available to borrow from your local library or eBook reader. If the local library is close enough you could even walk there!

- Prayer - John 14:26 But the Advocate, the Holy Spirit, whom the Father will send in my name, will teach you all things and will remind you of everything I have said to.

- Podcasts

- Blogs/Forums

- Social Media Groups – there are an abundance of Christian weight loss social media groups you can join, just google 'Christian weight loss groups'. Simple!

Prayer: *Lord, guide me in my learning, that I may grow in the knowledge of Your love for me and be encouraged to live my life as You would want me to.*

DAY 23 – DETERMINATION

1 Corinthians 9:24-26 Do you not know that in a race all the runners run, but only one gets the prize? Run in such a way as to get the prize. Everyone who competes in the games goes into strict training. They do it to get a crown that will not last, but we do it to get a crown that will last forever. Therefore I do not run like someone running aimlessly; I do not fight like a boxer beating the air.

Are you running your race aimlessly? Do you feel like you are beating the air, with no results? The scripture above says to 'Run in such a way as to get the prize.'

Think of your journey as a race. This doesn't need to be a fast race, it can be slow if that's what is achievable for you, but nevertheless your race has a start and a finish. Are you focused on the finish line, getting that crown that will last forever?

Physical and mental health is a great example of this. Being focused and determined in your physical and mental health has very long lasting results. Think about the freedom you will have (or even the increased freedom you are feeling already). Being able to be more active, more joyous, involved with others more, living healthier and longer, just to name a few!

Prayer: *Lord, remind me today of the strength I have that comes from you. Help me be determined to set myself up for a win, and focus on planning my journey.*

DAY 24 – EFFORT

Deuteronomy 6:5 Love the LORD your God with all your heart and with all your soul and with all your strength.

Effort isn't easy. That's why it takes EFFORT! Other words to describe effort are: exertion, stretch, struggle, attempt and strain.

2 Peter 1:5-10 says 'For this very reason, make every effort to add to your faith goodness; and to goodness, knowledge; and to knowledge, self-control; and to self-control, perseverance; and to perseverance, godliness; and to godliness, mutual affection; and to mutual affection, love. For if you possess these qualities in increasing measure, they will keep you from being ineffective and unproductive in your knowledge of our Lord Jesus Christ. But whoever does not have them is nearsighted and blind, forgetting that they have been cleansed from their past sins.

Therefore, my brothers and sisters, make every effort to confirm your calling and election. For if you do these things, you will never stumble,'

Phew, that's a long one, but well worth reading through. Faith, goodness, knowledge, self-control, perseverance, godliness, mutual affection and love... All of these can take effort, but it is promised that if we do these things, we will not stumble.

There is good news here though. The good thing about effort is if we practice it enough, things become 'effortless', meaning they require no effort at all, as they become part of who we are. Wouldn't it be great if we could demonstrate all of these things effortlessly? So, what does that take I hear you ask? Practice. Which takes effort.

Prayer: *Lord, guide me to love you with all of my heart and all of my soul and all of my strength. Let me practice faith, goodness, knowledge, self-control, perseverance, godliness, mutual affection and love until it becomes effortlessness.*

DAY 25 - BACK ON TRACK

Psalm 121

¹ I lift up my eyes to the mountains—
   where does my help come from?
² My help comes from the LORD,
   the Maker of heaven and earth.
³ He will not let your foot slip—
   he who watches over you will not slumber;
⁴ indeed, he who watches over Israel
   will neither slumber nor sleep.
⁵ The LORD watches over you—
   the LORD is your shade at your right hand;
⁶ the sun will not harm you by day,
   nor the moon by night.
⁷ The LORD will keep you from all harm—
   he will watch over your life;
⁸ the LORD will watch over your coming and going
   both now and forevermore.

Fallen off the bandwagon, or more to the point, the treadmill? Don't worry – that thing will keep turning its belt, ready for you to hop back on again.

God is watching over you, He will watch over your life and your coming and going – now and forever! Spend some time in conversation with God about your journey, think about what is working, what isn't working, why you've had a little hiccup, and how to get back on track.

Prayer: *Lord, help me to get back on track when I occasionally fall out of the race. My strength comes from You, and all things are possible in Your name!*

DAY 26 – STRONG FOUNDATIONS

Matthew 7:24-25 "Therefore everyone who hears these words of mine and puts them into practice is like a wise man who built his house on the rock. The rain came down, the streams rose, and the winds blew and beat against that house; yet it did not fall, because it had its foundation on the rock."

Proverbs 3:5 Trust in the Lord with all your heart, and do not lean on your own understanding.

Are your foundations strong? Are your goals attainable, and have you made the necessary changes in your life for them to be so? Are you sticking to them?

I am an avid gardener, and love being outside when the sun is shining. If I'm feeling a bit lazy though, I may buy a pot plant, dig a small hole, just pop the plant in and give it a bit of a water, then forget to water it for a few days. Not surprisingly, within a few days the plant is listless, if not dead already. If I just take a few extra minutes to dig a deeper hole, put some good soil in with it, give it some extra water, then water for a minute or two for a few days – the difference is amazing! I have a plant that is flourishing with life, and will even start flowering early!

We can look at ourselves as a plant. A few minutes in prayer, asking God for guidance in our day, and a few minutes meal planning or exercising everyday can build a strong foundation – and it really doesn't take as long as we think it does. Without strong foundations we ourselves can feel listless, and lose momentum. Just taking a few minutes out each day building on our foundations can make a world of difference.

Prayer: *Lord, remind me each day to spend at least a few minutes building strong foundations for my journey. Help me to flourish!*

DAY 27 – REST

Psalm 23:2-3 He makes me lie down in green pastures, he leads me beside quiet waters, he refreshes my soul..

God wants you to have rest, and our bodies need it to function properly.

Sleep promotes energy, clarity in our decision making when it comes to making healthier choices, positive moods and the ability to take in more information about the world around us.

There are no negatives when it comes to sleep, only positives, so make sure you are getting enough.

Set up a night time routine that gets your body into a nice easy pattern for sleeping. Eating or exercising too late at night can increase your adrenalin, making it hard for your body to get the rest it requires. Going to bed with heavy thoughts or just after studying can also hinder sleep.

End each day in quiet reflection, thanking God for the good things that have happened in your day - some days may be harder than others, but you will always find something to be grateful for.

Prayer: *Lord, I thank you for the gift of sleep. Remind me each day how important this is for my body, and my spirit. Help me to think on things I am grateful for.*

DAY 28 – CELEBRATE YOUR SUCCESS

Philippians 4:4 Rejoice in the Lord always. I will say it again: Rejoice!

There have been various studies that suggest celebrating your victories, no matter how small, increases endorphins which tell your brain that this is something your body would like to experience again!

So today let's set up a Celebration Ritual!

So every small victory, even if it's eating a healthy breakfast (which, personally, for me is a BIG victory!), do a little air punch, or give yourself a pat on the back; smile, and say 'YES!'. Thank God for allowing you this opportunity to take a positive step in your journey. And that's it, nothing long winded. Do this with each success and voila! You've created a Celebration Ritual!

You could surprise yourself with how positive you feel afterwards, and at how long this positivity lasts. Even if it feels awkward to begin with and you find you are laughing at yourself – hey, you're still laughing – that's got to be a positive, right?

Prayer: *Lord, I rejoice in you always! Thank you for allowing me the opportunity to celebrate victories with You by my side.*

DAY 29 – LIVING LIFE TO THE FULLEST

John 10:10 ".. I have come that they may have life, and have it to the full."

Jesus came so that you can have life, and that life to the full! So what are you waiting for?

What are Gods plans for you? What excites you about this?

There may be things that you haven't yet started that would make your life more fulfilled, or perhaps there are activities that you are only doing half-heartily. Look in to these today, and get moving!

Take time today to think about how you could be living your life more fully. In everything you do, give it 100%. And joyfully.

Don't feel joyful today? As the old saying goes, fake it until you make it. Right now, take a moment to put this book down, and force a smile for 15 seconds.

See, it works? You are probably still smiling.

This is what the Lord wants for You.

Prayer: *Lord, I pledge to give 100% to all that I do today, because Jesus gave his life for me, so that I may live mine to the fullest.*

DAY 30 – LET YOUR LIGHT SHINE

Proverbs 20:27 The human spirit is the lamp of the LORD that sheds light on one's inmost being.

This new found energy, joy and vibrancy - don't hide it. Smile at people as you pass them, let your light shine!

In Mark 4:21 Jesus says "Do you bring in a lamp to put it under a bowl or a bed? Instead, don't you put it on a stand?" Let's step up, and get on a stand! As friends and relatives notice your new happiness, they may comment on it. You can let them know that by relying on God, prayer, meditating on scriptures and setting up new habits you have found a new lease on life – that is definitely being an example of Christ.

Prayer: *Lord, as I have relied on You and grown through this journey with You by my side, help me be a light to others. Let Your love shine through me. Use me as a vessel for Your glory!*

SCRIPTURES TO MEDITATE ON

Romans 5:1-2 Therefore, since we have been justified through faith, we have peace with God through our Lord Jesus Christ, through whom we have gained access to faith into this grace in which we now stand.

Romans 12:2 Do not conform to the pattern of this world, but be transformed by the renewing of your mind. Then you will be able to test and approve what God's.

Psalm 86:11 Teach me your way, LORD, that I may rely on your faithfulness; give me an undivided heart, that I may fear your name.

Romans 2:13 For it is not those who hear the law who are righteous in God's sight, but it is those who obey the law who will be declared righteous.

Acts 5:29 Peter and the other apostles replied: "We must obey God rather than human beings!"

Deuteronomy 7:9 Know therefore that the Lord your God is God; he is the faithful God, keeping his covenant of love to a thousand generations of those who love him and keep his commandments.

James 4:3 When you ask, you do not receive, because you ask with wrong motives, that you may spend what you get on your pleasures.

1 Kings 8:61 And may your hearts be fully committed to the LORD our God, to live by his decrees and obey his commands, as at this time.

James 1:12 Blessed is the one who perseveres under trial because, having stood the test, that person will receive the crown of life that the Lord has promised.

Hebrews 13:6 So we say with confidence "The Lord is my helper; I will not be afraid. What can mere mortals do to me?"

3 John 1:2 Dear friend, I pray that you may enjoy good health and that all may go well with you, even as your soul is getting along well.

Matthew 18:20 For where two or three gather in my name, there am I with them.

John 15: 11 I have told you this so that my joy may be in you and that your joy may be complete.

John 8:32 Then you will know the truth, and the truth will set you free.

Jeremiah 33:6 "Nevertheless, I will bring health and healing to it; I will heal my people and will let them enjoy abundant peace and security"